Nelson Handwriting

Pupil Book 6

OXFORD
UNIVERSITY PRESS

Book 6 Scope and Sequence

Unit	Pupil Book Focus	Pupil Book Extra	Pupil Book Extension	Resource Book Focus	Resource Book Extension
1	Developing an individual handwriting style — copy country names	copy different handwriting styles	copy an extract	*ff, gg, jj, yy, bb, pp, qq,* practise adding loops to descenders; practise joining break letters; practise joining all letters	copy a poem, joining all your letters
2	Revising slanted writing — copy *ve* words	*scarf, wolf, loaf, knife, calf, wife* write words and their plurals	copy a nursery rhyme	copy the lower-case alphabet; write the plural of nouns ending in *o*	trace words and write their plurals; trace and complete sentences
3	Practising keeping letters in correct proportion — add prefixes	copy and complete a passage	copy a poem	*disbelief, disappointed, dishearten, disagreed, disguise, distracted* complete sentences	copy a poem
4	Practising writing fluently and legibly — add suffixes	*whistled, whining, crackling, staring* copy and complete sentences	copy a passage	*gaze, chuckle, injure, charge, decide, advertise, mumble* add *ed* or *ing* to verbs ending with a consonant plus e; copy and complete sentences	copy a poem
5	More practice forming and joining descenders — add vowel suffixes	*dutiful, bountiful, beautiful, naughtiness, happiness, craftiness* add suffixes to words ending in *y*	copy and complete similes	*yyyy, ffff, gggg, jjjj* practise writing descenders; add the suffix *ing* to words ending in *e*	add suffixes to words; copy a poem
6	Forming and joining the letter t — copy and complete word sums	*addition, subtraction, multiplication, evaporation, condensation, respiration* write correct spellings of words	copy and complete sentences	*ition, ation, ction, addition, subtraction, multiplication, evaporation, condensation, respiration* copy pattern, letters, words	copy a poem
7	Practising joining to and from the letter o — *hon, one, oto, cro, ono*	*telephone, phone, photo, geography, dolphin, microphone* write correct spellings of words	copy a poem	*one, ore, ogr, olp, oto, oph, tele, be, geo, dol, phone, phin, graphy, fore* copy letters; join letters to make a word	find *ph* words in a wordsearch
8	Practising punctuation — " " ! . ?	copy a passage	copy sentences; insert the missing punctuation	" , . ! ? copy punctuation; add punctuation to sentences and a passage	copy sentences; add the missing punctuation
9	More practice of slanting writing — *aeroplane, aerobatics, aerodrome, microdot, microscope, microscopic, transaction, transplant, transport*	*automatic, aquarium, aerodynamic, export, emigrate, european, preview, primrose, porter* underline the roots of words	copy and complete sentences	*bi, binary, biped, binoculars, tele, telephone, telegram, telescope, aqua, aquarium, aquaplane, aquatic* write slanted patterns and letters; copy prefixes and words	identify root words, prefixes and suffixes; copy words and underline the root
10	Practising writing capital letters — *whole alphabet*	copy sentences; add the missing capital letters	copy an extract	copy an alphabet shape poem	copy an extract; insert the missing capital letters
11	Practising spacing — *frightened, shouted, pleaded, lighthouse, determined, although*	copy sentences; add the missing speech marks and commas	write a short biography	copy words; underline the unstressed vowels	copy a poem
12	Practising writing instructions — *Check! Wait! Stop! Dismount! Choose! Watch! Steer! Disappear!*	copy instructions; add bullet points	design and make a leaflet	number and write instructions in the correct order	create a safety poster
13	Practising fluency, speed and legibility — *queue, question, queen, quench, quest*	copy and complete sentences	copy a diary entry	write patterns with increasing speed; copy sentences; find your writing speed	practise writing patterns; copy words quickly
14	Practising the diagonal join — *ent, ant, ence, ance*	copy and complete sentences	copy a passage	*distant, assistant, parliament, sufficient, conscience, convenience* copy patterns, words, sentence	copy and complete sentences; write two sentences

Unit	Pupil Book Focus	Pupil Book Extra	Pupil Book Extension	Resource Book Focus	Resource Book Extension
15	**Practising the horizontal join** *wri, wra, wro, wre*	copy and complete sentences	copy a tongue-twister	*w, c, g, k, t, wr, ck, ag, kn, th, write, gnat, sword, knock, castle* copy letters and words; underline silent letters	copy a poem; underline the silent letters; write a funny poem containing silent letters
16	**Practising forming letters at the correct height and size** copy connectives	make compound words	copy and complete instructions, using connectives	copy connectives	add *ly* to words; complete sentences using connectives; write instructions using connectives
17	**Leaving the correct space between letters** *ic, de, ad, as, ta, at, th, al, af, ef, fl, ff, wh, rl, rt, rd, rc, ow, we, re*	copy sentences	copy a poem	*sou, thr, all, aff, fec, ect, ice, eac, ace, ast* copy letters and homophones	copy a poem
18	**Practising joining to the letter r** *cracker, talker, shoulder, calculator, conductor, interior, calendar, popular, familiar*	arrange groups of words into alphabetical order	copy a poem	*er, ar, or* copy pattern, letters, words	copy and complete a biography
19	**Practising horizontal joins** *ary, ory, ery*	*dictionary, necessary, secretary, category, victory, history, cemetery, mystery, stationery* copy words; underline unstressed vowels	complete words using *ery* or *ary*; copy and complete sentences	*ory, ary, ery* copy pattern, letters, words	complete words by adding *ory, ary* or *ery*; write the plural of words
20	**Practising printing** *whole alphabet*	copy an advert in print	copy a poster in print	copy a fact sheet using print	copy a chart using print; copy and complete sentences
21	**Practising paragraphs** copy a paragraph	copy sentences; divide them into two paragraphs	copy sentences; divide them into three paragraphs	copy a paragraph	divide a passage into two paragraphs
22	**Practising writing double letters** *cc, oo, gg, ss, ff, ee, rr, mm, pp, ii, ll, tt*	*communicate, community, correspond, especially, immediate, sufficient, marvellous, programme* add in the correct double letters in words	copy a letter; lay it out correctly	write synonyms	copy a poem; underline words containing double letters
23	**Practising spacing within words** *by, my, fly, soldier, sufficient, variety, conscience, achieve, science*	sort *ie* and *ei* words by sound	copy a poem	*ien, iey, iew, iel, ief, achieve, receive, believe, perceive, field, belief* copy letters and words	copy a poem
24	**Ensuring letters are the correct proportion** *brave, hare, mouse, tortoise, solemn, lake, pancake, diamonds*	copy and complete similes	think of a simile to finish sentences	*lion, bee, snail, mouse, owl, ice, rake, peacock* copy and complete similes	copy similes; complete sentences with similes
25	**Practising presentation** draw borders	copy an address onto an envelope	design and make a party invitation	copy a certificate; decorate it with a border	copy a letter
26	**Practising fluency** copy pronouns	copy a passage, using pronouns	copy a passage	copy pronouns; write two sentences	copy a poem; write two sentences using pronouns
27	**Practising speedwriting** copy synonyms	turn notes into full directions	copy sentences in speedwriting	underline and correct spelling mistakes in a paragraph; rewrite the paragraph	edit a biography to correct the misspelt words; write a final draft
28	**Practising presentation** copy a poem	copy a poem, made up of kennings	write your own poem, using kennings	write an acrostic poem in the correct order; add a border	copy a poem

Joining all your letters

Focus

Everyone develops different styles of handwriting.
Some people make joins after the letters *b* and *p*.
Other people add loops from the letters *f*, *g*, *j* and *y*.

Write these words in your book.
Try joining all your letters except capitals.

Tokyo   Beijing   Uruguay   South Africa
Seychelles   Majorca   Paraguay   Tenerife
Malaysia   Fiji   Egypt   California

These sentences are written in different handwriting styles.
Copy the one you like best.

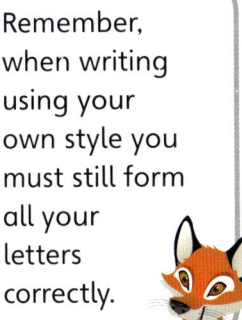

Remember, when writing using your own style you must still form all your letters correctly.

1 Tokyo was the most crowded place I visited on my travels.

2 Every morning the famous Bullet Train brought passengers into the city.

3 I saw amazing buildings, including an office block only two metres wide.

4 Each morning I joined hundreds of people exercising in the park.

Extension

Copy this extract into your book.
Remember to use your own preferred style of writing.

Hachiko was the pet dog of a professor at Tokyo University who used to meet his master off the train as he returned from work each day. After his master died while at work, Hachiko still turned up at the same spot, every day, for the next seven years. In admiration of this display of loyalty, the people of Tokyo had a statue built at the place where he waited.

From '*Full Circle*' by *Michael Palin*

Cryptographers solve ciphers.

Focus

Copy these words into your book.
Take care when you join the letter *v* to the letter *e*.
Angle your paper slightly to help you slant your writing.

vegetables	*vehicles*	*verses*
vests	*wolves*	*loaves*
knives	*thieves*	*wives*

> Joining the letter *v* to the letter *e* is tricky. Dip your pen down to the start of the letter, like this: *ve* not *ve*.

Extra

Write these words and their plurals in your book.
Slant your writing slightly to the right.

scarf =   wolf =

loaf =   knife =

calf =   wife =

> To make the plural of nouns that end in f or fe, we usually change the f or fe to v and add es, like this:
> wolf = wolves.

Extension

Copy this nursery rhyme onto lined paper.
Remember to form your letters at the correct height and size, slanting your writing slightly to the right.

As I was going to St. Ives,

I met a man with seven wives,

Each wife had seven sacks,

Each sack had seven cats,

Each cat had seven kits:

Kits, cats, sacks, and wives,

How many were there going to St. Ives?

Anonymous

7

Form your letters neatly and consistently.

Focus

A Adding these prefixes to a word gives it the opposite meaning. Copy them into your book.

un   de   dis   anti   il

B Add the prefix *un* to the words below.
Write them in your book.
The first one has been done for you.

un + happy = unhappy

kind

educated

helpful

identified

familiar

When you join the letter *f* to *a*, *u* or *i*, the horizontal joining line helps you form the next letter in the correct proportion, like this:

fa, fu, fi

Copy this passage into your book.
Choose the correct words.

A big mystery that has so far remained solved/unsolved is this: what are the identified/unidentified flying objects that have been seen in the sky? Some people have said that they are usual/unusual cloud formations. Ufologists usually/unusually claim that the Earth is being watched by alien intelligences. If so, what do these aliens want? Will we ever discover the truth?

Copy this poem onto plain paper.
Keep your letters in the correct proportion.

Unidentified Flying Object
There
in the night sky
with lights flashing
it swoops from high to low –
and straight away it's identified
as an unfamiliar
UFO!

By Ronald Kay

Fluent writing flows quickly!

Focus

A Copy these words into your book.
Remember to join your letters.

stare	*whine*	*crackle*	*whistle*
stared	*whined*	*crackled*	*whistled*
staring	*whining*	*crackling*	*whistling*

To add a suffix to a word ending with *e*, drop the *e* if the suffix begins with a vowel: *stare + ing = staring*. If the suffix begins with a consonant, we usually keep the *e*: *stare + d = stared*.

Extra

Use a word from the **Focus** activity to finish these sentences.
Copy the sentences into your book.
Remember to write fluently and legibly.

Looping your descenders will help make your handwriting fluent.

1 The wind _____ through the trees.

2 I could hear a dog _____ in the distance.

3 Suddenly I heard the log fire _____.

4 Then I saw two eyes _____ at me.

Extension

Copy this passage into your book, using fluent and legible handwriting.

There were strange whining noises and odd whistling sounds that Imran couldn't identify. He felt a shiver run down his spine. What could the noises be? He crept forward. Suddenly he heard a loud moan from beneath his feet. Could there be dungeons under the castle floor? If so, who or what was down there?

Remember to use your best handwriting when you want to present neat, careful work.

Dad is persuading me to learn how to cook!

Focus

Suffixes beginning with vowels are called vowel suffixes.
Add these suffixes to create a new word. Write the new word.

achieve + ing =

average + ing =

chase + ing =

communicate + ing =

interfere + ing =

persuade + ing =

> The letters *g, j y, f, p* and *q,* are descenders. The tails of these letters fall below the line. You can join descenders if you make a loop like this: *gyj*

To add a suffix to a word that ends in *y* (where the *y* sounds like *e* in *tea*), change the *y* to an *i*. Like this: *happy* + *ness* = *happiness*.

Add the suffixes to these words. Make sure the descenders sit on the line and the tail falls below the line.

duty + ful =   bounty + ful =

beauty + ful =   naughty + ness =

happy + ness =   crafty + ness =

Extension

> Be careful with *f*. It is a tall letter and its tail also falls below the line. Practise joining it to the next letter like this: *fu*

Similes describe things by saying something else. Copy these similes and choose the correct word to complete the sentence.

1 The old woman's face was as *wrinkled* / *wrinkly* as elephant skin.

2 The moth *danced* / *dancing* around the lamp like a ballerina.

3 The cat was as *fluffy* / *fluffiness* as a woolly hat.

4 The monkey scratched her head, looking like a *puzzling* / *puzzled* child.

Billy worked out the addition sums.

Focus

A Copy these letters. Remember, the letter *t* is not as tall as the other ascenders.

tion   tion   tion   tion   tion

B Copy and complete these word sums.

accommodate + tion = accommodation

appreciate + tion =

communicate + tion =

exaggerate + tion =

> Remember, slanting your writing will help you write quickly and fluently.

Extra

All of the words below are misspelt.
Write the correct spellings in your book.
Slant your writing slightly to the right.

adition   subtracsion

multiplicashun   evapouration

condenseation   respirasion

Extension

Copy and complete these sentences.
Choose the correct word.

1 Water formed from vapour is called
   condensation/evaporation.

2 An animal with a backbone is called a vertebrate/mammal.

3 When we absorb food it is called dissolve/digestion.

4 A mammal/predator is an animal that suckles its young.

5 Friction/fraction is when an object rubs against another.

A phonograph is an early form of record player.

Focus

A Copy these letters into your book.

hon   one   oto   cro   ono

B Copy these words into your book.

phone   phono   photo

micro   copy   gram

C Join together two words from **B** to make three new words, like this: *microphone*. Write these words in your book.

Ensure the joining line from the letter *o* creates a space so the letters do not touch each other.

In most words *ph* sounds like **f**. The words below have been misspelt. Write the correct spellings in your book.

telefone   fone   foto
geografy   dolfin   microfone

> The join from the letter *o* to an ascender is made near the top of the letter.

Extension

Copy this poem onto plain paper. Put guidelines underneath to help you. Remember to join carefully from the letter *o*, ensuring the letters do not touch.

The Elephant

The elephant carries a great big trunk;
He never packs it with clothes;
It has no lock and it has no key,
But he takes it wherever he goes.

Anonymous

It's the Romans!

Focus

A Copy these punctuation marks into your book.
Look carefully at their size and height.

" " " "   ! ! ! !   . . . .   ? ? ? ?

B Copy these sentences into your book.

"Help!" shouted the villagers.

"Look out! She's coming!" cried the soldiers.

Copy this passage into your book.

"Who are you?" the soldier asked.

"I am just a farmer. I live in the village," the boy stuttered.

"Lead me there at once!" the soldier demanded.

Copy these sentences.
Insert the missing punctuation.

Who s she   asked a soldier

She s the wife of Prasutagus   her

name is Boudica   replied another

She s a famous Celtic warrior

a third warned

Slanting your handwriting will help you write quickly and neatly.

Focus

Copy these words into your book.
Remember to slant your writing slightly to the right.

aeroplane	*aerobatics*	*aerodrome*
microdot	*microscope*	*microscopic*
transaction	*transplant*	*transport*

A Roots are words, or parts of words, to which prefixes and suffixes can be added to make words from the same family.

Copy the words below, slanting your writing.
Underline the root of each word.
The first two have been done for you.

> When slanting your handwriting, remember all your letters must have the same slant.

<u>auto</u>matic   <u>aqua</u>rium   aerodynamic

export   emigrate   european

preview   primrose   porter

Extension

Copy and complete these sentences, choosing the correct word.
Use a dictionary to check the meaning of unfamiliar words.

1 Many women learned to fly *aeroplanes/aerodromes* during the Second World War.

2 Aeroplanes were used to *transport/transplant* troops and drop agents behind enemy lines.

3 A *microdot/microscope* is a tiny photograph of a coded message.

Mary Seacole was a famous Victorian.

Focus

Here is each capital letter with its lower-case version.
Copy these letters three times into your book.

Aa Bb Cc Dd Ee Ff Gg Hh Ii Jj
Kk Ll Mm Nn Oo Pp Qq Rr Ss Tt
Uu Vv Ww Xx Yy Zz

These sentences show what Mary Seacole did.
Copy them into your book. Add the missing capital letters.
The first one has been done for you.

> Remember, capital letters are the same height as ascenders.

I knew the hospitals in the Crimea were filthy and rat-infested.

1 *i volunteered my services to the army, but i was rejected.*

2 *so i travelled to the crimea and opened the british hotel.*

3 *wherever i went i took medicines and food for the soldiers.*

Extension

> Remember, capital letters are break letters.

This is an extract from Mary Seacole's account of her own life, her autobiography. Copy this extract into your book.
Make sure your capital letters are as tall as ascenders.

The first day that I approached the wharf (at Balaclava) a party of sick and wounded had just arrived. Seeing a poor artilleryman I ran up to him at once, and eased the stiff dressing and well was I rewarded when the poor fellow's groans subsided into a restless easy mutter.

From '**Wonderful Adventures of Mrs Seacole in Many Lands**'

"Can I row with you?" Grace Darling pleaded.

Focus

A Copy these words into your book.

frightened   shouted   pleaded

lighthouse   determined   although

B Copy this sentence into your book.

Although Grace was frightened, she pleaded with her father to let her row with him to rescue the survivors of the shipwreck.

Extra

A A conversation can be written down exactly as it is spoken, by using speech marks. A comma is added before the last speech mark, like this:

"I can see people on the rocks and in the water,"
shouted Grace.

B Copy these sentences into your book.
Leave an equal space between your letters and an equal space between your words.
Add the missing speech marks and commas.

> Remember, speech marks are written at the same height as ascenders.

1 *We can't just leave them to drown sobbed Grace.*

2 *Grace, the sea is very rough said her father.*

3 *If we both go, we can row together pleaded Grace.*

Extension

When someone else writes information about the life of a real person, it is called a biography.

Use the notes below to make a short biography of Grace Darling. Write it in your book in your best handwriting.

> Remember, letters must not touch each other, like this:
>
>   ✓

Grace Darling (1815–42)

Her father was a lighthouse keeper.

In 1838, a boat called the 'Forfarshire' struck rocks near the lighthouse.

Grace and her father rowed out in a small boat to rescue the survivors.

They had to make their trip through huge waves.

They became famous for their great bravery.

Cyclists should always wear a helmet.

Focus

A Copy these instructions into your book.

Check!   *Wait!*   *Stop!*   *Dismount!*

Choose!   *Watch!*   *Steer!*   *Disappear!*

B Think of four more instruction words.
Write them in your book.

Extra

These instructions are for cyclists wanting to turn right.
Copy them into your book. Add bullet points.

Remember to space out your instructions to make them clear.

Check the traffic, signal, and move to the centre of the road.

Wait until there is a safe gap in the traffic before turning.

When it is safe, turn right.

Extension

Design and make a leaflet called 'Buying a bicycle'.
Plan your pages. Decide where your writing will go.
Will you use print writing or slanted and joined writing?

Write down the title of the leaflet.
You need to include this advice for buyers:

- Check the cycle is the right size for you.

- Check the saddle and handlebars are the right height.

- Check the lights and reflectors are working properly.

- Check the brakes and gears are working efficiently.

- Check the tyres are inflated to the right pressure.

People queued to see Tutankhamun's treasures.

Focus

A Copy this letter pattern.

ueue   ueue   ueue   ueue

B Match the two sets of letters below.
Write the correct spellings in your book, like this: *queue.*

que	tion
ques	e
quen	n
quee	ch
queu	st

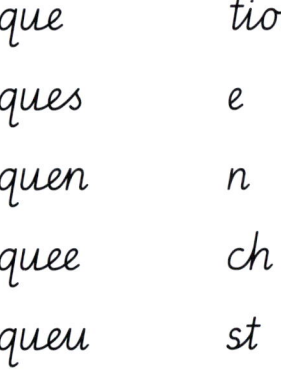

Joining and slightly slanting all of your letters will help you to write fluently and with speed.

C How many words beginning with *qu* can you write in five minutes?
Remember to join all your letters to help you write quickly and fluently.

Extra

A Read these words.

unique   plaque   cheque

B Copy these sentences and insert the correct words.

1   This was a _____ expedition to discover Tutankhamun's tomb.

2   Carter was given a _____ to help finance the foreign trip.

3   A _____ was awarded in his name.

Extension

A Copy Howard Carter's diary entry onto lined paper. Remember to slant your writing to help you write fluently and with speed.

4th November 1922

Lord Carnarvon accompanied me as I searched for the ancient Egyptian boy king, Tutankhamun. I had managed to persuade him to finance one final trip as I was desperate to achieve my lifelong quest to find the tomb. According to the foreman, Ali, we were now within two days of reaching the sealed door. I suddenly began to appreciate how close we were to making a discovery.

B What did Howard Carter find inside the tomb?

UNIT 14

Practising the diagonal join

Focus

A Copy these letters. Join your letters carefully using a diagonal joining line.

ent ent ent ent

ant ant ant ant

ence ence ence ence

ance ance ance ance

Remember, the diagonal join joins letters from the bottom of one letter to the top of the next.

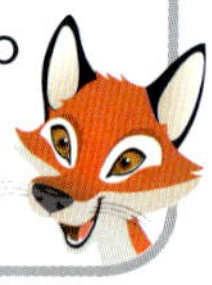

B Copy these words into your book.

distant
assistant
conscience
convenience
hindrance
nuisance
parliament
sufficient

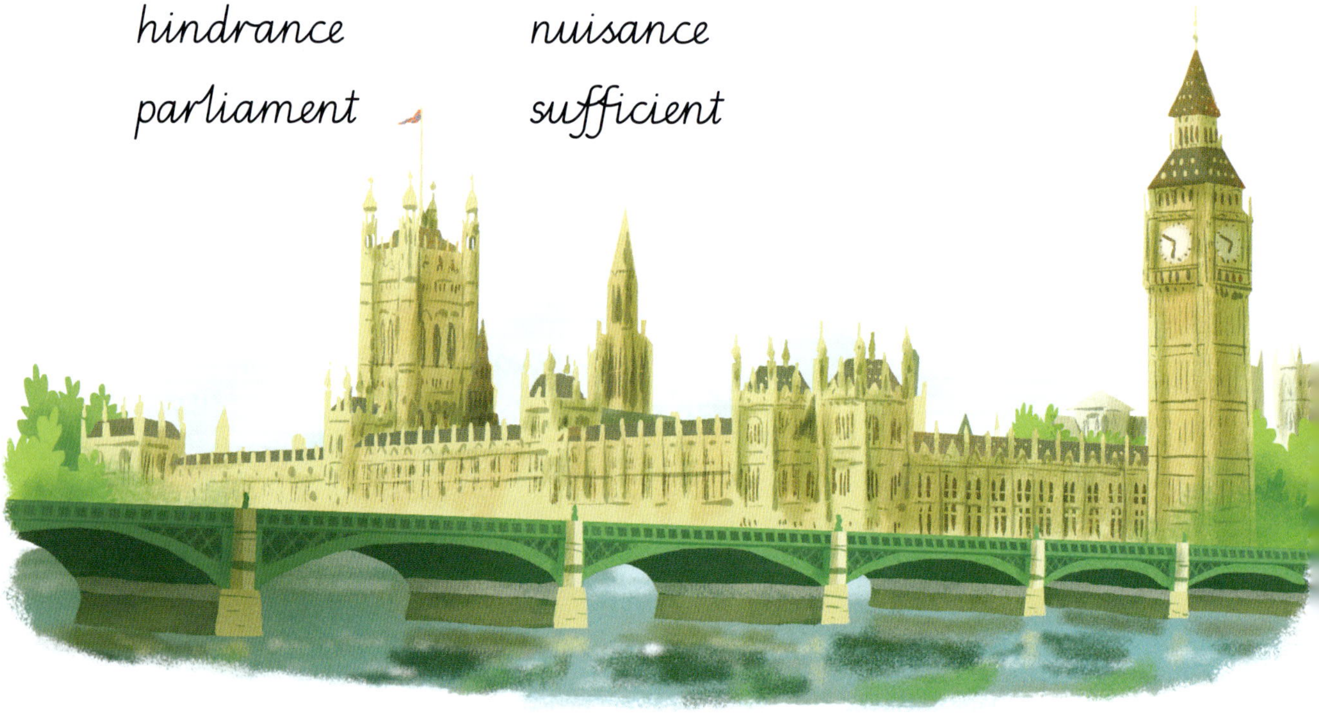

Copy and complete these sentences.
Choose the correct words to fill the gaps.
Remember to form and join your letters correctly.

1 Our local _____ store is very close to our house.
(conveniance/convenience)

2 The shop _____ was very helpful.
(asssitent/assistant)

3 She found _____ bread to make forty sandwiches.
(sufficient/sufficant)

4 My baby brother was more of a _____ than a help.
(hindrence/hindrance)

Extension

Copy this passage into your book.

Although the shop assistant knew the supplies were
insufficient, they would have to last until the end of the day.
It was a nuisance, but there was nothing she could do about it
now. She just hoped that she didn't have too many customers
wanting to visit the convenience store that day.

Focus

A Copy these patterns into your book.

MMMMMMM   MMMMMMMM

ooooooooo   ooooooooo

papapapa   papapapa

MMMMMMM   MMMMMMM

amamam   wewewewe

B Copy these words into your book.
Make sure all of your letters are the correct height and size.

vehicles   loaves

average   communicate

interfere   appreciate

queue   conscience

C Copy these words into your book.
Make sure your writing is slanted slightly to the right.

sufficient   hindrance

parliament   nuisance

persuade   exaggerate

invasion   soldier

Copy these words into your book using fluent and legible handwriting.
Make sure you are making the joins correctly.

my	wait	stop	check
safe	push	left	gap
famous	prefer	unkind	her
helpful	stare	leaves	struck
whistle	crackle	noise	crew
bicycle	castle	flows	fire
rough	pleased	launched	coast
familiar	usual	island	tanker
although	shipwreck	efficient	cyclist
disappear	Egypt	Fiji	Tokyo

Extension

Copy this poem into your book.

The city mouse eats bread and cheese;
The garden mouse eats what he can;
We will not grudge him seeds and stocks,
Poor little timid furry man.

From 'The City Mouse and the Garden Mouse' by *Christina Rossetti*

I like wrestling with my brother.

Focus

A Copy these letters into your book.
Join the letters carefully using a diagonal joining line.

wri   wra   wro   wre

B Copy these words into your book.
Take care when joining *r* to *e*. The join dips down
to the start of the letter.

wreck   wrestle   wrist

write   wrapper   wrong

When joining
from *w* to *r*,
the joining line
helps ensure
the letters do
not touch.
Like this: wr
not wr.

A silent *w*
usually goes
before *r*.

Extra

Copy these sentences and insert the correct words into the gaps. Remember to join your letters carefully.

The joining line helps ensure you space your letters correctly.

1 *Anthony Horowitz is a very good write/writer.*

2 *When I grow up I want to be a professional wrestle/wrestler.*

3 *The worm wriggled/wriggler along the path.*

Extension

Copy this tongue-twister onto lined paper.
Remember to use a horizontal joining line after the letters *o*, *r* and *w*.

A right-handed fellow named Wright,

In writing "write", always wrote "rite"

Where he meant to write right.

If he'd written "write" right

Wright would not have wrought rot writing "rite".

35

November 5th is Bonfire Night and some people watch fireworks.

Focus

Copy these connectives.
Write your letters at the correct height and size.

but	*because*
besides	*after*
although	*alternatively*
whereas	*whoever*
whatever	*then*
therefore	*thereafter*

> Remember, the letters *b*, *d*, *f*, *h*, *k* and *l* are ascenders. They are almost twice the size of small letters. Take care with the letter *t*, as it is not quite as tall as the other ascenders.

Compound words contain two separate words, which, when joined together, make a new word. Like this: *further + more = furthermore.*

Join a word from each box below to make a new word.
Write the new word in your book, taking care to form your letters at the correct height and size.

further		ever
how	**+**	more
mean		fore
there		while

= **?**

Extension

A Copy these instructions onto lined paper.
Choose the correct connective word from above to complete the sentences.

> Remember, ascenders just touch the top line.

1 Always keep fireworks in a box; _____ make sure the lid is kept shut.

2 Matches can burn your fingers _____ use a taper to light fireworks.

3 Fireworks are fun to watch _____ you must always be careful with them.

B Write two more instructions using connectives from above.

We heard the herd coming!

Focus

A Joining letters correctly helps you leave the correct space between letters. Practise joining the letters below, using the four joins.

ic	*de*	*ad*	*as*	*ta*
at	*th*	*al*	*af*	*ef*
fl	*ff*	*wh*	*rl*	*rt*
rd	*rc*	*ow*	*we*	*re*

> Homophones are words that sound the same but are spelt differently and have different meanings.

B Copy these words. Take care to join your letters correctly, leaving the correct amount of space between letters.

devise	*device*
threw	*through*
farther	*father*
heard	*herd*

Extra

Copy these sentences into your book.
Remember to leave the correct amount of space between
your letters and between words.

1 My father and I had a wonderful time on our Safari holiday.

2 The herd stampeded across the desert.

3 We could still see the animals through the dust their
   hooves kicked up.

Extension

Copy this poem onto plain paper. Take care with your presentation.
Remember to join your letters correctly, leaving the right amount of
space between letters and between words.

The Importance of Rain – A Hindu poem

If clouds withhold the promised rain
Hunger and distress in the world reign
If clouds impart the bounteous rain
It restores hunger's gnawing pain.

Chandra Thiagarajan

A computer is a superior form of calculator.

Focus

Copy these words into your book.
Remember to take your pen to the top of the letter *r*.

cracker	*talker*	*shoulder*
calculator	*conductor*	*interior*
calendar	*popular*	*familiar*

> Remember to join to the top of the letter *r*, like this: *er, ar*

A Arrange these groups of words into alphabetical order. Write them in your book.

1 computer   newspaper   customer
  stranger   builder   helper

2 superior   radiator   doctor
  motor   sailor   instructor

3 burglar   particular   similar
  popular   calendar   regular

Extension

Copy this poem onto lined paper.
Take care to join your letters correctly.

My Granny's an absolute corker,

My Granny's an absolute cracker,

But she's Britain's speediest talker

And champion yackety-yacker!

By *Kit Wright*

Mary wrote a letter using her new stationery.

Focus

Copy these letters into your book.
Use horizontal joining to help space your letters.

ary	*tary*	*nary*	*mary*
ory	*tory*	*nory*	*mory*
ery	*tery*	*nery*	*lery*

> The horizontal joining line joins *r* and *y*, and *o* and *r* from the end of one letter to the start of the next.
> Like this:
> *ry, or*

Unstressed vowels are vowel letters we do not sound, or do not sound very distinctly. Copy these words. Put a line under the unstressed vowels.

dictionary   necessary   secretary

category   victory   history

cemetery   mystery   stationery

Extension

A Use a dictionary.
Complete each word by adding –ery or –ary.

nurs_____   ordin_____   batt_____

compliment_____   prim_____   revolution_____

B Choose the correct spellings to complete these sentences.
Remember to join your letters carefully.

1 My baby brother has just started nursery/nursary school.

2 The car battery/battary was flat this morning so we had to walk.

3 I go to Fisher Pond Primery/Primary School.

4 The school is not an ordinery/ordinary school.

5 My teacher was very complimentary/complimentery about my handwriting today.

Print letters are easy to read.

Focus

A Copy the print alphabet into your book.

Aa Bb Cc Dd Ee Ff Gg Hh Ii Jj Kk Ll Mm Nn
Oo Pp Qq Rr Ss Tt Uu Vv Ww Xx Yy Zz

B These words use lower-case print letters.
Copy these words into your book.

run	swim	snorkel	dig
running	swimming	snorkelling	digging
runner	swimmer	snorkeller	digger

Carefully written print is good for adverts and posters because it stands out.

Copy this advert onto plain paper. Use the print alphabet.

DREAMLAND EUROPE

So much to see and do:

- swim
- snorkel
- dig for gold
- run The Dreamland Challenge

Extension

Copy this poster onto a sheet of plain paper.
Fill in the activities section.
Make sure you use the print alphabet.

Remember to draw pencil lines on your paper to help you make your letters the correct size and height.

STEP INTO A WORLD OF MAGIC

Come to

DREAMLAND EUROPE

So many activities to enjoy:

_____

_____

_____

_____

 21, rue Bougainvillaea
12345 Marseille, France

Paragraphs help you to organise your writing.

Focus

Copy this paragraph into your book in your best handwriting.

The Loch Ness Monster is believed to live in a loch, or lake, in Scotland. Some people claim they have seen it. Some have even taken photographs of a strange dark shape.

> Remember to indent the first word of each paragraph.

Write these sentences in your book.
Divide the sentences into two paragraphs.
Remember to start each new paragraph on a new line
and indent the first word.

The Abominable Snowman, or the Yeti, is said to be a huge, hairy, human-like creature living in the Himalayas. In 1957, an explorer set out on a Yeti hunt after five local people had been killed. But he didn't find the Yeti.

Extension

Write these sentences in your book.
Divide the sentences into three paragraphs.

In 1951, a climber took photographs of huge footprints in the snow. Could these have been made by the Yeti? An expert on snow explained that footprints made by a smaller animal could have started to melt in the midday sun and frozen again at night. Each time this happened, the footprints would have got bigger until they looked enormous. High in the mountains, the air is very thin. The lack of oxygen can make people imagine strange things.

The audience applauded the marvellous music.

Focus

A Copy these letters into your book.

cc	cc	cc	oo	oo	oo	gg	gg	gg
ss	ss	ss	ff	ff	ff	ee	ee	ee
rr	rr	rr	mm	mm	mm	pp	pp	pp
ii	ii	ii	ll	ll	ll	tt	tt	tt

Take care to form your letters the correct height and size.

B Copy these words into your book.
Underline the letters someone might forget to put in, like this: *accommodate*.

accommodate   accompany   according

apparent   appreciate   applause

referred   preferred   transferred

Look carefully at these words.
All of the double consonants have been taken out.
Think carefully about where any double letters should be.
Write the correct spellings in your book.

comunicate   comunity   corespond   especialy

imediate   suficient   marvelous   programe

Copy this letter onto plain paper.
Use guidelines underneath the paper to help you.
Take care to set your letter out correctly.
Remember to add your signature, address and the date.

Dear Jimmy,

I wanted to write to you immediately to tell you that we thoroughly enjoyed the excellent play. For an amateur production it was brilliant! I didn't recognise you in the soldier's uniform and we thoroughly enjoyed your marvellous singing too.

It could have been disastrous when the equipment collapsed and the yacht failed to emerge from the wings, but the show must go on!

I especially liked the bit when the lightning made the vegetables fall off the plate in the restaurant. According to Julia, she hasn't laughed so much in ages!

Despite the long queue for tickets, I am glad you persuaded me to go. I will definitely recommend the play to my friends.

Yours sincerely,

How high can a fly fly?

Focus

Copy these words into your book.
Make sure your letters do not touch each other.

by	my	fly
soldier	sufficient	variety
conscience	achieve	science

> Use a joining line to help ensure the correct spacing between your letters.

A Look again at the words in the **Focus** section.
Underline the words that have an **i** sound written with *ie* or *y*.

B Below are five of the seven different sounds made by *ie* or *ei*.
Copy the table and insert the following words into the correct column.
Remember to write your letters so they do not touch each other.

hygiene   variety   patient   receive   leisure

sounds like	ie words	ei words
ee as in creek	hygiene	
y as in my		
e as in best		leisure
u as in hunt		
oo as in boot	review	

Extension

Copy this poem onto lined paper. Take care to join your letters correctly.
This will help ensure you leave the correct space between the letters in each word.

The Fly

Little Fly,
Thy summer's play
My thoughtless hand
Has brush'd away.

Am not I
A fly like thee?
Or art not thou

A man like me?
For I dance,
And drink and sing,
Till some blind hand
Shall brush my wing.

From '**The Fly**' by *William Blake*

The cat was as quiet as a mouse.

Focus

A Copy these words into your book.
Ensure your letters are the correct height and size.

brave   hare   mouse   tortoise

solemn   lake   pancake   diamonds

B Look again at the words above.
Underline the sounds you cannot hear, like this: *mouse*.

Copy these similes into your book. Choose the correct words to finish the similes.
Make sure you write your letters at the correct height and size.

As slow as a *hare/mouse/tortoise*.

As cold as *ice/custard/pasta*.

As quiet as a *horse/mouse/zebra*.

As brave as a *rock/jelly/lion*.

Extension

Think of a simile to finish each sentence.
Copy these sentences into your book.
Make sure your letters are in the correct proportion
to each other.

Remember,
the letter t
is not as tall
as the other
ascenders.

1 The cat was as quick as _____.

2 The dog was as cool as a _____ as the
cat leapt towards him.

3 The cat's eyes sparkled like _____.

4 Mrs Smith's hat was as flat as a _____
after Tom sat on it!

UNIT 25

Practising presentation

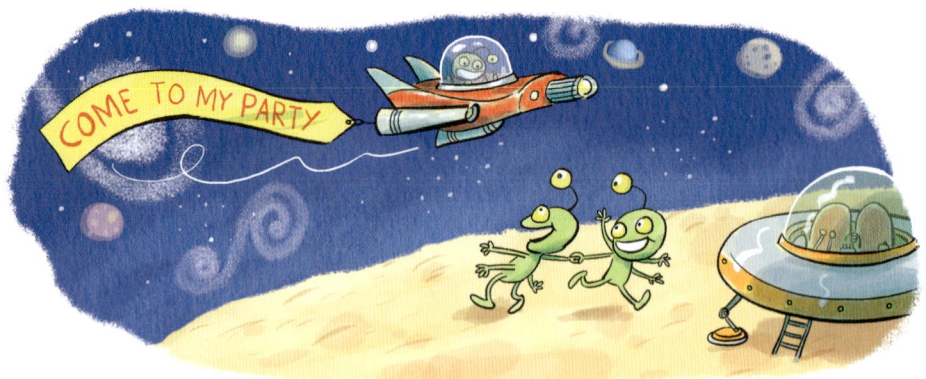

Focus

Practise drawing different borders on a piece of paper. You can use borders when you want to present a piece of writing attractively.

Draw some guidelines in pencil on your paper. This will help you keep your letters the correct height and size and your writing straight across the paper.

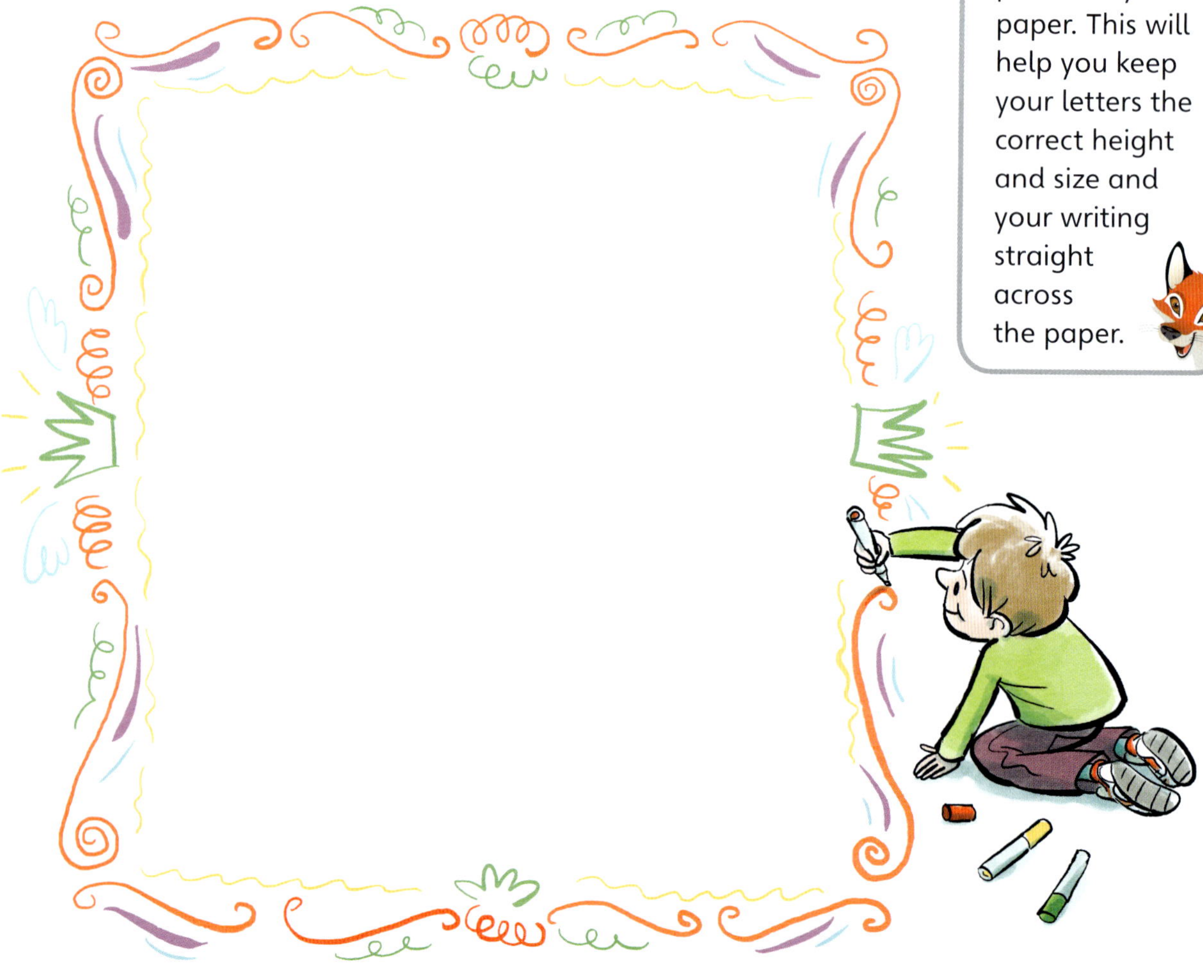

Practise writing the address on an envelope.
Remember to plan where you will write the address before you start.

> To Miss Christine Hamley
> 29 The Spinneys,
> Chipping Aston,
> Bournemouth,
> Dorset
> BH17 2RD

Extension

Use these instructions to design and make an invitation to 'An aliens fancy dress party' on a piece of plain paper. Don't forget to say who the invitation is for, what it is to, the day, the time, where it will take place, and who it is from.

> You are less likely to smudge your work if you start at the top left-hand corner.

1   Plan where your writing will go.
2   Pencil in the borders and colour them.
3   Lightly pencil in some guidelines. Use a ruler to make sure the lines are the same width apart.
4   Write in your text.
5   Rub out the pencil lines.

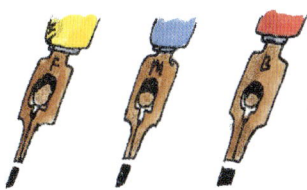

This was written with a fine pen nib.
This was written with a medium pen nib.
This was written with a broad pen nib.

Narcissus loved to admire himself.

Focus

Copy these pronouns into your book.

he	you	we	them	all
her	your	me	they	it
him	yours	she	their	us

> Remember, joining your letters helps you to write quickly and fluently.

Extra

Copy this passage into your book.
Sometimes use the pronouns *him* or *he* instead of 'Narcissus' to make the passage easier to read.

Narcissus was very handsome. Many people came to Narcissus and said they loved Narcissus but Narcissus treated them all the same. Narcissus rejected them.

Extension

Copy this passage into your book.
Make sure your writing is fluent, joined and legible.

Narcissus thought he was beautiful. He wanted to share his life with someone equally beautiful.

One day, as he was walking in the forest, he felt he was being followed. "Show yourself!" he shouted. "Show yourself," a voice replied. The words were the same, but the voice was so beautiful. "Let me see you," he pleaded. "Let me see you," the voice replied.

A nymph called Echo appeared. But Narcissus rejected her when he realised that all she could do was repeat what had just been said.

Focus

When speedwriting, it can be quicker to use a shorter word in place of the original word. These words are different ways of saying *dig*, *buried* and *box*. Copy them into your book as quickly as you can.

dig	excavate	tunnel	investigate	probe
buried	entombed	hidden	immersed	covered
box	case	trunk	container	chest

These are quickly written notes about the location of some treasure.
Write the directions out in full in your book.
Make sure your handwriting is neat.

Wlk 6 stps nth of lghthse.

Tke 10 stps est.

Go cave.

Fllow undgrd tnnl.

X mrks spot.

Copy these sentences into your book in speedwriting.

1 *There is a steep cliff around the cove.*

2 *The treasure chest is under the rock.*

3 *There are gold coins in the box.*

4 *The pirates land on the beach.*

5 *They excavate beneath the rock.*

6 *They find the treasure and carry it up the cliff.*

> Use the shortened form of words (*there's*) and some different, shorter words (*box*, *dig*) if you think it will help you to write quickly.

Focus

Copy this poem into your book.
Make it look as attractive as you can.

Marmalade

A ginger tom
name of Marmalade
shaved his whiskers
with a razor-blade

Last mistake
he ever made.

By *Roger McGough*

> Remember, it is easier to slant your letters to the right if you turn your paper at a slight angle.

Extra

A kenning is a way of describing something without saying what it is. This poem is a list of kennings. Copy it into your book.

A toe-nibbler

A dark-dreamer

A paw-padder

A floor-scratcher

A warm-sleeper

A night-creeper

A fur-cleaner

A flea-finder

A mouse-hunter

A house-minder

A secret-hoarder

A china-breaker

A four-foot-lander

Think about presentation. Plan where your poem will begin and end. Will you start your poem at the side of the page, or will you write it in the middle?

'Cat' by *Rachel Myers*

Extension

Write your own poem about a kitten using kennings. Start by making some quick notes.
Then write a first draft in your book.
Use your best handwriting for the final copy.

Remember to add a border to decorate your poem.

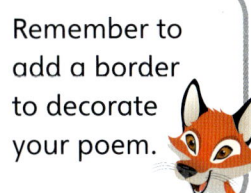

CHECK-UP 2

Focus

You should now be able to join your letters using the four joins.
Copy these words into your book.

and	so	dinner	digging
biped	bicycle	happy	unhappy
illegible	illegal	transport	transplant
snorkelling	unfamiliar	California	Tenerife
counteract	countermove	lorries	crosses
before	therefore	furthermore	box
whined	whistled	counterfeit	counterfoil
otherwise	parasol	cliffs	bipartite

You should now be able to write quickly, neatly and legibly.

A Copy these words into your book.

investigate

identified

otherwise

furthermore

B Write the word *investigate* as many times as you can in 30 seconds.

C This sentence contains all the handwriting joins.
Copy it into your book in your best handwriting.

The police began to investigate why the box was buried near the cliffs.

D Practise writing the sentences above quickly, neatly and legibly.
Time yourself to find out how quickly you can write the sentence.

Copy this poem onto plain paper.
Use guidelines underneath. Set the poem out
carefully and neatly, remembering all you
have learned about presenting your work.

Marbles in my pocket,

Blue and green and red,

And some are yellow-golden,

And some are brown instead.

Marbles in the playground,

Big and little ring —

Oh, I like playing marbles,

But that's a different thing.

Marbles in my pocket,

Smooth within my hand,

That's the part that's nicest;

Do you understand?

Marbles in my pocket

To rattle when I run!

For winter days are here again,

And marble-time's begun!

From '**Marbles in my Pocket**' by *Lydia Pender*